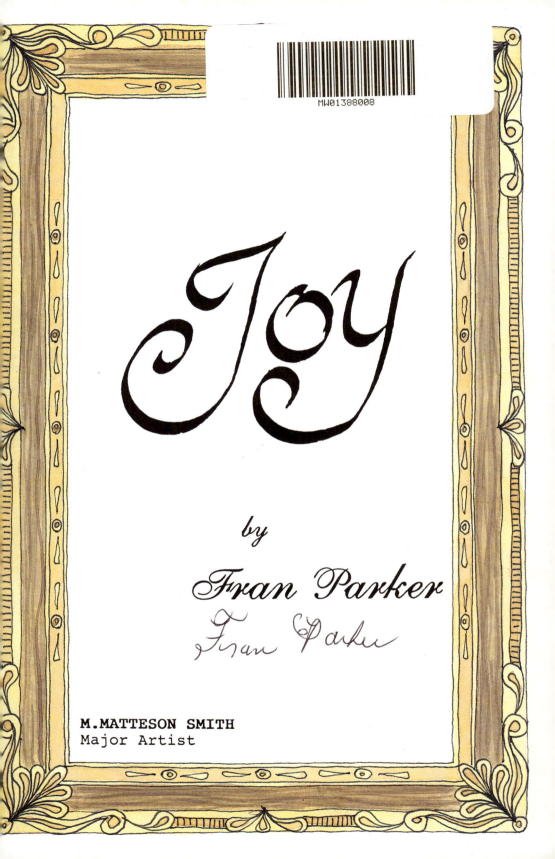

Joy

by

Fran Parker

M. MATTESON SMITH
Major Artist

ISBN 0-933193-13-0

Published by TarPar Ltd., 1202 Harding Avenue, Kinston, NC 28501
Library of Congress Control Number: 2001130599
Printed in China
Copyright: 2002

All rights reserved. No portion of any art,
or prose may be reproduced without the
written permission of the publisher or
the Author.

Dear Reader,

Since I often wonder just why an author chooses the subject, the title, or the words for a book, I thought I would share with you my reason for doing all of the above. I could say "it just happened," but in truth it all evolved over several years. I have been blessed to have a great deal of JOY in my life with ever so many people that seemed to pile up JOY upon me with their humor, good vibes, and old fashion love that all these thoughts and words just started pouring out of my brain onto paper. Readers of my works have told me that what I write is exactly what they too are feeling and wished to express but just didn't quite know how; therefore, they have a fond empathy and personal reaction in the over and over reading of the phrases.

It is really neither poetry or prose, but a mixture of thoughts that are conveyed from me to you on a printed page.

Brenda Woodley, an English teacher at Kinston High School in Kinston, North Carolina, edited these pages for me, and I got a pleasant glow from her comments... "Reading your book on the theme of joy, has brightened my weekend and my existence. You have found what Bhrigu Varuni in his ancient book on Indian Hindu teachings concluded...'the reality that underlies everything perceived by the sense is joy.' Congratulations on writing such a joyous book of poetry!"

I sincerely hope all my readers will share her comments. It has been a joy to share them with you.

                                        Fran

September 11, 2001 was a day never to be forgotten with its fill of violence, turmoil, and nonjoy. On that day, the familiar world ceased to exist, touching hearts around the globe. Our task now is clear. We must build a bonfire of love, service, sacrifice, well-rooted patriotism, and determination that will burn for centuries as the eternal JOY and a purpose of uniting this world in peace under GOD. . . .your God, and mine. We must set a goal for a world that is a JOYOUS place in which to dwell together in brotherhood.

(To my readers: This addendum was written after the book was already packed for the printer. . .it just had to be included. Peace to each of you.)

                                                                Fran

JOY comes in many forms
We meet it every day
The chirp of a bird,
The warmth of the sun,
Hot breakfast coffee,
A job well done.

      JOY'S face has many facets
      And none should be overlooked;
      The smile of a child
      A hug from a friend,
      The blooms of the flowers,
      The list never ends.

Looking with awe at the big
      City lights,
You find JOY watching the trains
      On the tracks.
There is pleasure with the antics
      Of squirrels and the capers of fawns.
A drive down the road,
      The homes around the bend.

      The light from the lighthouse
      Sends JOY, peace, and hope
      To all mariners within its scope;
      Rays are spread in the darkness
          Of the night
      And into the brightness of the dawn.

BELIEVE IT.......JOY ABOUNDS!!!!!

I'm not a snowbird,
    I'd fly south if I could,
But when a day deals you snowflakes
    Take heart and relax.
The crackle of a fire, the warmth of a cup,
    The smell of a stew and not much to do
Gives time for reflections,
    To read and regroup.
That mantle of white is not gloom—
    It's a joke!
It's slippery, it's sliddy…it's
    A day made for fun!
The sun shines tomorrow!
    Today, just ENJOY!!!

> "You have changed my sadness into a joyful dance: you have taken away my sadness and surrounded me with JOY"
>
> Psalm 30:11 (TEV)

Joy is so totally contagious!
It is like
A wild fire blown by fierce winds,
A giggle that grows into uncontrollable laughter,
A night blooming cereus that won't stop until
In full bloom,
The wide spread ripple that grows from the
Very small pebble tossed into a pond.

Joy continues to grow—
Spread—
Infect—
And we are all the better for it.

> "JOY descends gently upon us like the evening dew, and does not patter down like a hail storm"
>
> Richter

DREAM...not just those wild things
You cannot control in your sleep, but
Real DREAMS...
         MEGADREAMS...
              BEAUTIFUL DREAMS...
                   WONDERFUL DREAMS...

Accept that ninety-nine percent of them won't
come true, but enjoy DREAMING those tiny fragments
that filter through your vivid imagination, weaving
patterns within your brain, and making spellbinders
of your waking hours.

The course of your life could change if you followed
your DREAMS, a life catapulted into joy and
happiness. New scientific experiments would begin
and horizons would expand to the maximum.

Take a walk...even in the rain and clear your mind
of all those cobwebs. Make room for your
DREAMS. Escape the prison walls of current reality.
Break out in JOYOUS laughter and learn that
DREAMING AND JOY walk hand-in-hand.

NEVER
   EVER
      STOP
         YOUR
            MIND
               FROM
                  GROWING
                     AND
                        DREAMING!!!
THEY JUST MIGHT COME TRUE!!!

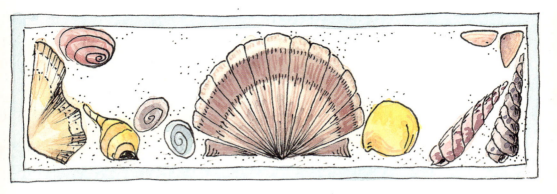

There is JOY of course in just the
 fantastic game of chance of being alive,
But the real excitement comes from
 JOYOUS living and how you choose
 to spend your days.
Each new day you are given JOY
 in the morning and restful,
 peaceful JOY at night.
You have a chance to find JOY in
 achievement and to learn a
 lesson from failure.
I guess you can say there is JOY
 in not being finished yet. . .
Like polishing a table or weeding
 a garden, washing dishes, or
 saying your prayers.
"Morning people" are thrilled to
 open their eyes, early. . .and take
 in the new day, be it sun, rain,
 fog, or clouds
That gives them the feeling of
 newness and the anxious urge
 to get going.
The "night creepers" hate to say
 goodnight to the moon, the stars,
 the frogs in chorus, the crickets,
 and the late show,
But they end the day with the same
 feeling of tired elation in
 having receive JOY, having
 given out a portion of JOY
 and, gratefully having shared in the
 pleasure.

Enchanted Moments

Enchantment seems to hold an invisible aura that takes on a mystical feel. It is heart-skipping a beat time. . .the fast beat of the pulse time
. . .the placement of a non-erasable computer chip into the brain time!
Can you shut your eyes and recall such moments and places?

I CAN!!!

Small things actually, but so much a part of each of our lives.
        Trinkets. . .yet extremely tangible
        Trifles. . .but so very permanent
        Trusts. . .meant to last forever.

A small gold cross, which will last and be worn forever, even though the giver has long been gone.

        The surprising arrival of a dozen red
        roses whose scent last only a scant
        moment in time, but the sender remains
        mine.

The rustle of blue net ruffles on the most delicious of gowns that brings a far away, dreamy, look to the eyes, even though the creation is long gone.

        A summer moonlight cruise where confidences and
        confessions were shared and remain a chapter of spellbound
        JOY.

Favorite songs shared across the miles, creating flashbacks and wide grins into a time that once was.

NEVER. . .NO, NEVER. . .LET GO OF YOUR MYSTICAL ENCHANTING MEMORIES

I heard a woodpecker on a
    tall sapling tree
Tapping out a long, loud message,
I saw a hummingbird make
    its first summer visit
To the sweet, red, life giving
    nectar bottle,
The beautiful cardinal family,
    showing their superiority,
    was vying for first
Place at the feeder,
And my heart filled with JOY
    knowing the winged creatures
Of nature had chosen our yard
    for their home.

I then thought of shut-ins whose only
    outlet to the world
Is the limited vision they can gain
    through a window pane.
Surely the many birds are their very
    special friends
With their singing, flapping, flying
    and tip-toeing
To bring a smile to the frail lips
    and special JOY into their lives.
Those feathered smaritans that build their
    architectual houses
And flights after flight fill them with
    their collection of gourmet seeds
Are truly the carriers of JOY, as
    they serve both man, birds, and God.

I heard a woodpecker on a
tall sapling tree
Tapping out a long, loud message,
I saw a hummingbird make
its first summer visit
To the sweet, red, life giving
nectar bottle.
The beautiful cardinal family,
showing their superiority,
was vying for first
Place at the feeder.
And my heart filled with JOY
knowing the winged creatures
Of nature had chosen our yard
for their home.

I then thought of shut-ins whose only
outlet to the world
Is the limited vision they can gain
through a window pane.
Surely the many birds are their very
special friends
With their singing, flapping, flying
and tip-toeing
To bring a smile to the frail lips
and special JOY into their lives.
Those feathered smartians that build their
architectual houses
And flights after flight fill them with
their collection of gourmet seeds
Are truly the carriers of JOY, as
they serve both man, birds, and God.

The Dry Spell

There seems to come a "dry spell" in all of our lives.
a time when new, rich, spontaneous thoughts and ideas
        just
            don't
                flow.

Plans stay status-quo. Interest gets put on hold. We
come to the conclusion we are totally brain-dead.
        So much to do.
                So little incentive.
                      What could be wrong?
                              Is there going to be an answer?

AH, YES!
Look at the dessert, dry as a bone, but in due time the
rains will come and there from the dust and hard baked soil
the flower will bloom.
        New growth will appear.
                Life giving color does return.

To end the empty feeling of mind and spirit takes just
one bolt of lightning. Meeting one new person, taking
just one road never traveled, hearing just one new
tune
        Could be the atom we needed...
                The flash to awaken the system....
                The quick, bright impulse to
                        Unglue the wheels of creativity.

Ideas once again jump around like a convention of
                Mexican jumping beans.!
                      Once again JOY comes with
                          Work, planning,
                              And originality!!

Sing now.... laugh now....
    Tell me how you feel now....
Love me.... touch me....
    Tell me what you plan, now.

Share now.... play now....
    Look into your future now.
Together now.... loving now....
    Taking our lives forever now.

I can think of nothing better
    Than all my life with you.... to
    enjoy.... now.

> "Let them thank the Lord for His steadfast love, for His wonderful works to the sons of men. And let them offer sacrifices of thanksgiving and tell of His deed in songs of JOY."
>
> Psalm 107:21-22

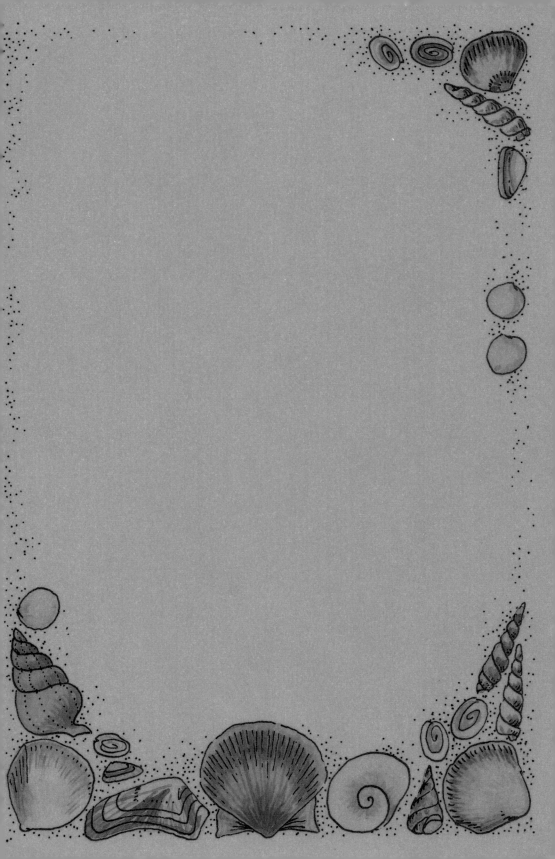

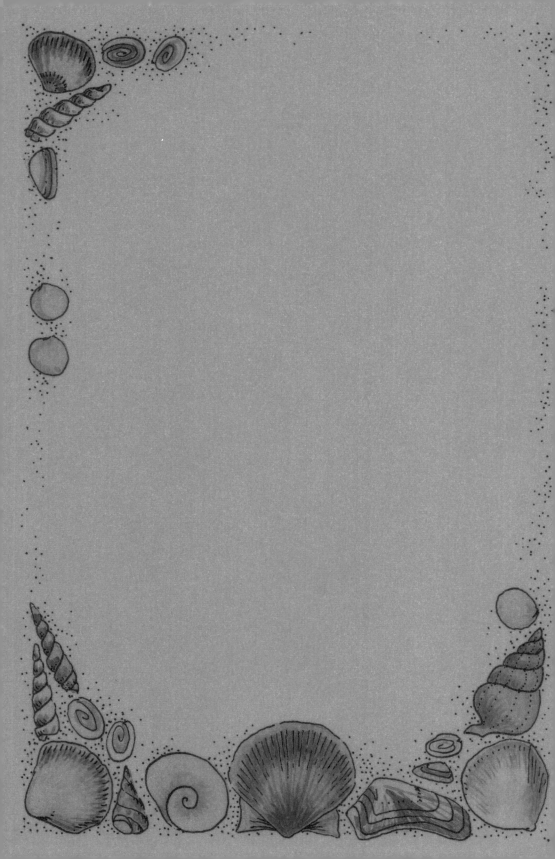

Today I received a hug from the sky
        and a kiss from the sea.
To top that off, there was a wink from
        the wind
And a smile from the blue cloudless sky.
Mixed in with all these gifts
        I found that there was
JOY in silence
        JOY in sound
                JOY in darkness
                        JOY in the light
What a glorious way to spend a day!!
What an exceptional way to enjoy life.

Well, whatever
> Happened to things we
>> Use to know and
>> Things we use to do?

Jump ropes, cart wheels and riding a bike
> With "no hands!!"
>> The feel of squashing mud between
>> Our toes, all day suckers and
>> "Mary Janes!"

Flying kites, playing marbles, or chasing butterflies?
> Having a day peppered with merriment,
> Cotton candy, and JOY!

Crackers in bed for breakfast, a "no-hair-curler"day,
> No make-up and no phone calls!
>> A day with no errands and no
>> Must-do-, to-do, list!

A day to think neat thoughts, to put funny names on
> The odd shaped clouds in the azure blue sky!
>> A glorious, stolen day for fun,
>> regrouping, and getting "it" all together
>> again!

A time to know me, so that upon my
return to that world of today
I will know that I am a
better person for tomorrow.

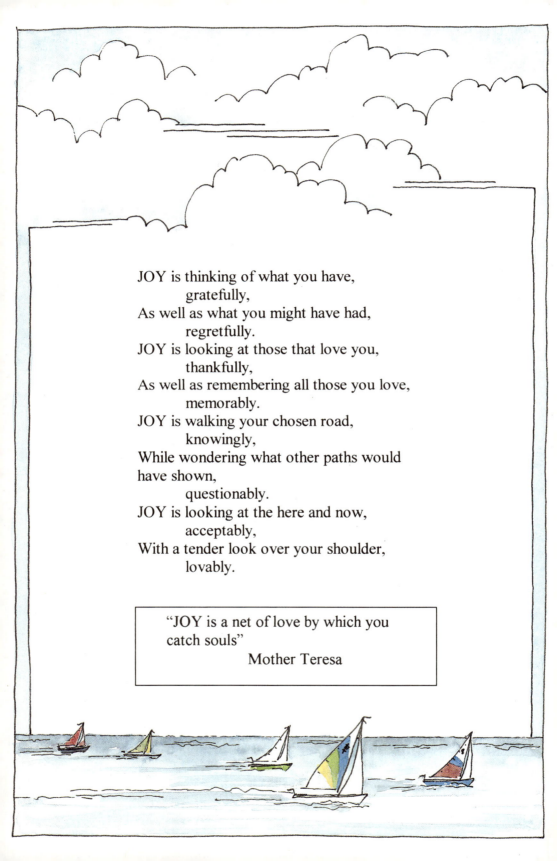

JOY is thinking of what you have,
    gratefully,
As well as what you might have had,
    regretfully.
JOY is looking at those that love you,
    thankfully,
As well as remembering all those you love,
    memorably.
JOY is walking your chosen road,
    knowingly,
While wondering what other paths would have shown,
    questionably.
JOY is looking at the here and now,
    acceptably,
With a tender look over your shoulder,
    lovably.

> "JOY is a net of love by which you catch souls"
>   Mother Teresa

Do take a moment to pity the poor, incurable,
romantic! They have a disease with no possible
cure. Watch carefully for these symptoms.

They gather dust-balls under their beds in
exchange for making a tin of cookies for a
shut-in.

Their cluttered closets show no rhyme or reason,
yet flowers bloom in their gardens, abundantly,
season after season.

The ironing basket looks like Pikes Peak,
but a friend is sick and a lonely child needs
love and affection.

They are never too busy to lend a helping hand
to anyone and never too tired to share a very late
meal with a friend or companion.

These poor incurables drop their JOY all over
town, spreading the smile germs, and the happy
feelings.

        To be pited???

            NEVER!!!

JOY came in a most unexpected way today.
A dreary rain greeted the opening of my eyes
nudging a slow awakening to the day with the
promise of nothing more to offer than mundane chores, a day to get some
"put-off-till-the-last minute" things marked off the perpetual list.

The morning dragged on as predicted. . .
piddling about with clothes to wash, making a stew for the
evening meal, a few phone calls. . .all kept company
with the melodic strains of favorite CD's in the background.

By chance, I took a peek out the window just to
check on the weather and, "pon my soul" SNOW!!
Beautiful, wee cotton balls were tossing and blowing, falling
helter-skelter to start their ground coverlet. A winter
wonderland. . .a JOY unsurpassed. . .a kick into a spiritual
world!

This phenomenon had not been on the weather
man's map of even a probability, yet here it was a possibility
in earnest. . .a happening! For a Southern lady with a past
New England residence, these fluffy flakes flooded my brain
with memories in the same tumbleweed effect as the
snowflakes bombarded each other in their flight to earth.

A cup of hot tea added to the pleasure of this "cup overflowing"
moment, and praying it would not stop and
continue to cover my world in white satan,
 I became a nostalgic snow watcher.
All chores, mundane or necessary,
were put on hold for the duration
of this happy, delightful, and
totally unexpected gift of JOY!

JOY can be measured in many opposite, yet
    funny, ways.

The moment you reached your diet goal. . .
    and the reward of munching on a candy bar!

Your long planned for guests driving up. . .
    and the moment they drive away!

The votes are all counted and you have won. . .
    versus the day you are no longer responsible!

The time you start your dreamed of job. . .
    the day you can retire and walk away!

The anticipation of decorating for Christmas. . .
    And the day the tree comes down!

The fun of having the grandchildren visit. . .
    And the relief when they wave goodbye!

The packing for the long dreamed of cruise. . .
    And the day you get back home!

There is JOY in everyday life, in everything
    You do, and everywhere you go.

    Your job is to look
        for the JOY
            and share it!

It was a morning to reach out and dust
the air. Humidity surrounded the earth like
the mist from an awesome waterfall.
The smells of the early morning melted
into the low land salty marshes. Could
I, even in my euphoria, realize that spring
had at last returned!

        The winter silhouettes that very
        recently were all scrawny sticks had been
        shopping for their new wardrobes
        of delicate pinks, blues, yellows,
        and whites. The world was
        invited to a mammoth fashion show
        with many graceful models.

JOY had returned to our neighborhood!
The winter gloom and cares were taking
off like a child hiding from given chores.
I talked back to the birds, I skipped
among the flowering boughs, and I gave
my thanks with a smile. The spirits soared
with the sheer JOY of sharing, once
again, this seasonal miracle.

It was a morning to reach out and dust
the air. Humidity surrounded the earth like
the mist from an awesome waterfall.
The smells of the early morning melted
into the low land salty marshes. Could
I, even in my euphoria, realize that spring
had at last returned!

The winter silhouettes that very
recently were all scrawny sticks had been
shopping for their new wardrobes
of delicate pinks, blues, yellows,
and whites. The world was
invited to a mammoth fashion show
with many graceful models.

JOY had returned to our neighborhood!
The winter gloom and cares were taking
off like a child hiding from given chores.
I talked back to the birds, I skipped
among the flowering boughs, and I gave
my thanks with a smile. The spirits soared
with the sheer JOY of sharing, once
again, this seasonal miracle.

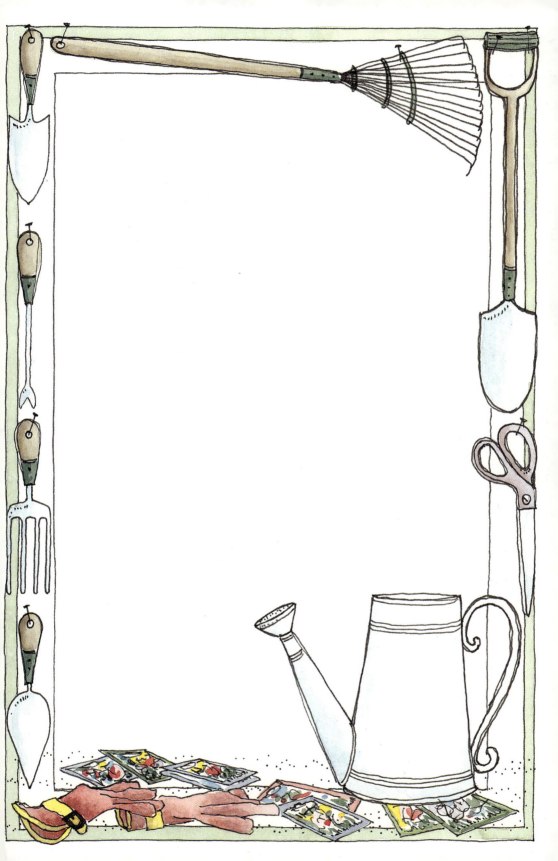

I can see the world of beauty
as well as the dinginess of the slums
but I am blind to the needs of others.

> I can hear all of the glorious sounds
> of family, friends, and nature,
> but I do not hear the cry of those in need.

I can smell the fragrance of a rose and
the aroma of freshly baked bread,
but I turn away from the smell of poverty and mire.

> I can speak in an assertive voice over a
> cause I believe in and utter sympathetic words
> to those I love,
> but I fail to speak up for those that
> need a voice of concern.

I can touch my children, lovely silks and satins and
objects of personal greed,
but I shrink back from touching the unclean, the sick,
and those in distress.

> All of these gifts of the five senses are
> God's blessing and a gift to me. . .yet I
> Take each of them so very much for granted.

How long does it take a person to learn
the JOY of sharing each and every one
of these blessings with others?

JOY pops you in the face, heart and mind at any time of
your life...day or night...spring or fall...expected or
totally unannounced...earned or a complete gift,
prince or pauper, each are on the receiving end
of JOY.
    It is not bought, not earned.
    It just arrives.

JOY can come in a variety of sizes. Some bundles
have the very smallest of ears, and you are sure they
will never be large enough to hear the music of a
symphony or the cheers of the crowd.

    Some bundles have the very tiniest of fingers
    that you know will never be able to reach an
    octave on the piano or catch a football pass.
    Some bundles have such minute toes that the
    idea of ever standing en pointe as a ballerina,
    or hiking a mountain trail is out of the question.

JOY can be found sharing a crackling fire with family
and friends close at hand, the recovery of a loved one,
    the first steps of a child,
        the first word, the first tooth,
a fresh baked apple pie,
    the smell of bread rising,
        fresh strawberries, birthdays,
            church and dinner on the
            grounds.

    All these JOYS are the many colorful
    patches sewed into the quilts that
    cover us with warmth, giving
        us the structure of our lives.

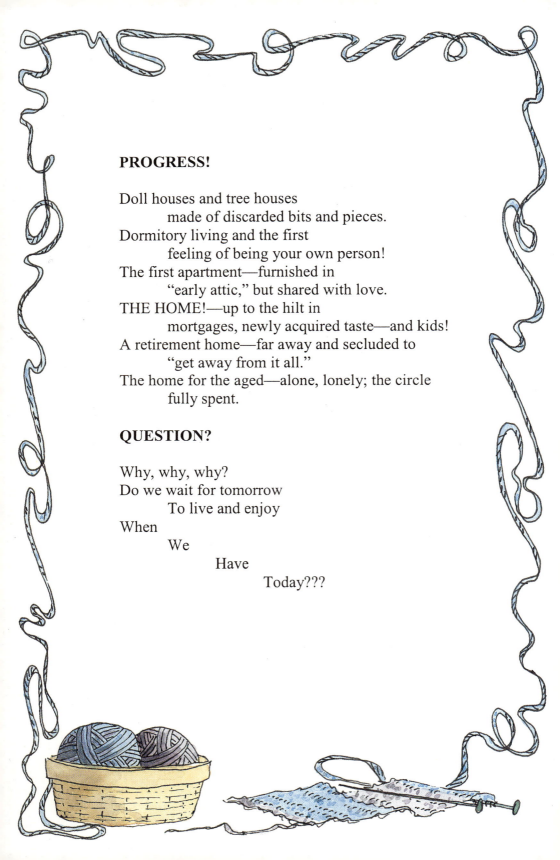

PROGRESS!

Doll houses and tree houses
      made of discarded bits and pieces.
Dormitory living and the first
      feeling of being your own person!
The first apartment—furnished in
      "early attic," but shared with love.
THE HOME!—up to the hilt in
      mortgages, newly acquired taste—and kids!
A retirement home—far away and secluded to
      "get away from it all."
The home for the aged—alone, lonely; the circle
      fully spent.

QUESTION?

Why, why, why?
Do we wait for tomorrow
      To live and enjoy
When
        We
              Have
                      Today???

Ah—JOY!!
The narcotic feeling of not having to do anything
is labeled "V.A.C.A.T.I.O.N.!!
Time to read a book, the simple pleasure of
taking a nap, the conscience sinfulness of
eating—or drinking—whatever you want!
The leisure of no-time to be anywhere, the total
emersion of soul and spirit into your chosen
spot in all the world, and then, like the caterpillar,
spring forth into the butterfly, cleansed,
refreshed, and overjoyed.

> "My brothers and sisters, whenever you face
> trials of any kind, consider it nothing but
> JOY."
>
> James 1:2 (NRSV)

Ah—JOY!!
The narcotic feeling of not having to do anything
is labeled "V.A.C.A.T.I.O.N.!!
Time to read a book, the simple pleasure of
taking a nap, the conscience sinfulness of
eating—or drinking—whatever you want!
The leisure of no-time to be anywhere, the total
emersion of soul and spirit into your chosen
spot in all the world, and then, like the caterpillar,
spring forth into the butterfly, cleansed,
refreshed, and overjoyed.

> "My brothers and sisters, whenever you face
> trials of any kind, consider it nothing but
> JOY."
> James 1:2 (NRSV)

There are times I feel that artists are
the true souls of our world with their
canvas,
  oils,
    paints,
      brushes,
        talent.
They bring into our homes the places
and images we have wanted to visit.
A field of flowers,
  a snow capped mountain,
    the pounding sea,
      the pensive face of our Lord.

An old man's thoughts can be read, and
felt through the work of the artist. Some
artist are long gone,
  many awaiting their turn
    to be applauded,
      appreciated,
        discovered.

But—wait. . .Are we not all artist?
Weavers,
 Quilters,
  Singers,
   Musicians,
    Potters,
     House Painters,
     Florist,
     Teachers
      Nurses,
        Indians Chiefs
Indeed, we all add our share
of beauty to the world just
by being ourselves!

I looked over my shoulder
    and what did I see?
        Ten billion things I'd wanted to do.
        So many things I had planned to be.

The blueprint of my plan
    just reached a crescendo.
        It all seemed so simple
        when the drafting first started.

Why, I had college, careers,
    love and marriage all sorted
        into a time frame of logic. . .
        or so it seemed then.

Now, over my shoulder
    I recall "might have beens."
        So, cancel those schedules, grab your
        suitcases and go. To heck with it all!

IT'S TOMORROW YOU KNOW!

> "In the JOY of little things, the heart finds it's
>   morning and is refreshed."
>
>   The Prophet

I'm just the plain vanilla
> but you are the chocolate sauce.

I'm only the empty vase
> but you are the flowers.

You add the fragrance to
> the cut glass bottle of perfume.

Just as you are, you are truly
> the spice in my life.

You fill my life with the helium
> that allows me to float like a balloon

Up into the stratosphere to
> watch the exciting world below.

Ordinary day by day, face to face,
> friends are never heroes,

We tend to look to the stars of the
> many medias or to the playing

Fields of the sports world, but
> who are they? Unknowns, except by face.

We live with our heroes, unspoken praise
> to those we love and those who help
> us daily.

Every day has at least one special minute
> that leaves a special memory.

It's up to each of us to take those
> moments, remember them well and
> enjoy the sharing of a chocolate sundae,
> the vase of fragrant summer flowers,
> the fine French perfume, and the
> view from our own
> kitchen windows.

From my lofty perch on an airborne bird,
        as I travel to and fro,
I look down on hundreds of "puff-a-belly"
        clouds drifting through the sky.

It gives me time to ponder,
        to let my mind freely flow
To places I have been and
        to friends that I have known.

For hours I am held captive
        in this big bird in the sky.
Nothing to do. . .nowhere to go,
        so I just bath in memories of you.

Those happy days and laughing hours,
        with a few sad tears sprinkled in,
Just seem to make the carousel of
        life an exciting place to be.

Our frantic pace and busy days seldom
        Schedule any time for just thinking.
This is a gift of time itself to smile
        at the surrounding clouds
                and have a chance to dream
                those dreams
                      yet to come.

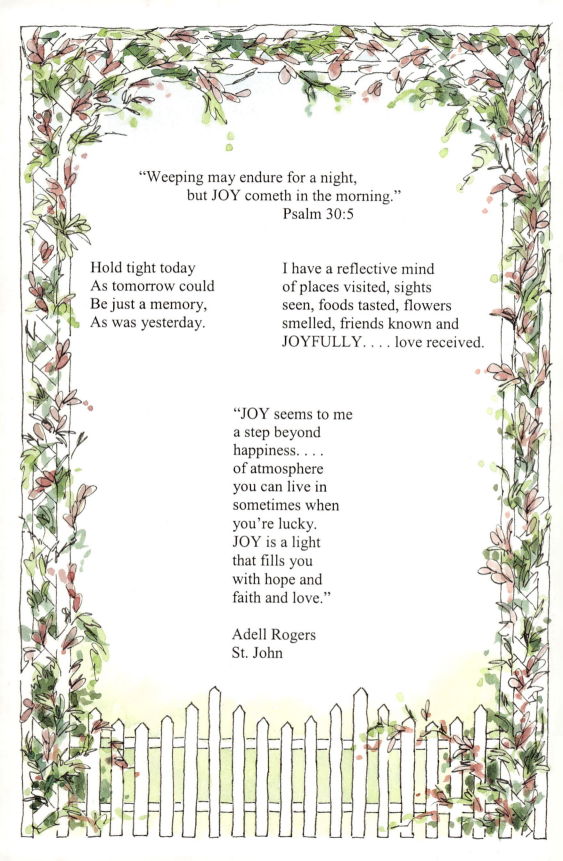

"Weeping may endure for a night,
but JOY cometh in the morning."
Psalm 30:5

Hold tight today
As tomorrow could
Be just a memory,
As was yesterday.

I have a reflective mind
of places visited, sights
seen, foods tasted, flowers
smelled, friends known and
JOYFULLY.... love received.

"JOY seems to me
a step beyond
happiness....
of atmosphere
you can live in
sometimes when
you're lucky.
JOY is a light
that fills you
with hope and
faith and love."

Adell Rogers
St. John

JOY can be found in the drop of rain
    that brings a long slow shower
       . . . .canceling all your outdoor plans.

    JOY can be found in a child's tearful cry
        That seems unceasing, even spiteful
        and an immediate threat to your sanity.

        JOY can be found in that small amount of milk,
            coffee, juice or ink that turns into
            a gallon as you clean the floor.

            JOY can be found in the loss of a longtime
                family pet that one hour is under your feet and the
                next gone forever.

Can it be possible to say. . .or even think, that there
could be JOY in the aftermath of a fire, grief, or a
weather caused disaster?

True, there is no hilarious, immediate or
profound jubilation over any change of
plans, agenda, or life style. . . .

        However. . .in the looking back,
           in the recollection,
                in the effect on your total outlook on life. . .

    YES! There was JOY. There is JOY
        in all the trivial, small-or large-events
           of your life. Each is just another lesson
                that builds your character, enhances your
                    spirit and your acceptance of the day's events.

As you build your life there is—there must be—
    JOY in every thing, every day, every hour.

What can make a smile so bright
That you know for sure all is going right.
    What can give a tingle that the sun shines within
    and you can feel moonbeams right through your
    skin?

What prompts you to do a somersault bringing
    chuckles to all around;
What gives you that sure-fire notion that
    only goodness abounds?
Let us see. . .
There is the dream of one day shooting par
and watching children put lightning bugs in a jar!
The fun of planning and packing for a trip
to watch your team win the championship.
The grand satisfaction of paying off the mortgage
and watching your little ballerina on stage. . . .
Then as years roll by, walking that same lass
    down the isle
In all her bridal beauty and style.
Receiving a long overdue pay raise that speaks
to your work with silent praise.
Silently watching your family when they have
    their change to shine
and pinching yourself to wonder. . .are they
    really mine?
Slipping away from all of life conglomerations
to read a book in total relaxation.
Turning into your own driveway with lights
    bright in the dormers
knowing that inside that home love grows ever
    warmer.

Don't loose those moments. . .be they ever so
small. These make your smile brighter, your
days JOYOUS, and your life abundantly rich.

Frances Carr Parker

- ❖ loves to dabble in sharing her thoughts and love with others

- ❖ loves her retired doctor husband, four grown kids, five grandkids, two "in-laws," her sister and family

- ❖ finds joy in decorating their home, planting flowers, and adores hosting parties

- ❖ takes pride as a Salem College graduate, Watts Hospital Dietetic Internship and California Western University post graduate

- ❖ takes pride in her many professional honors and 30 years as a dietitian and director of Child Nutrition Programs

- ❖ anything connected to Duke University!

- ❖ rejoices in her legion of friends and those that have molded her life

- ❖ delights in her church, clubs, attempt at golf, and being captain of her own 46' Chris Craft Aqua Home

- ❖ is humble and proud to share this JOY with readers across the miles

M. Matteson Smith

- ❖ loves watercolor, the sea, and pizza
- ❖ has earned a B.F.A., almost a Master's and awards
- ❖ respects creativity, integrity, and self-sufficiency
- ❖ hates cold weather, turnips, and whining
- ❖ adores the beach, painting and chocolate
- ❖ dislikes small places, small minds, and bugs
- ❖ enjoys biking, baking, and sleeping late
- ❖ teaches watercolor lessons, classes, and workshops
- ❖ wears jeans, many different hats, and a wedding ring
- ❖ has three kids and a kind heart

Martha Weeks Daniels

The delightfully different art on pages 35, 81, 85, 92 were done by the talented Martha Weeks Daniel who is a graphic designer, illustrator, and head of Daniel Design Associates, an advertising/design agency in Rocky Mount, NC. She is a graduate of St. Mary's College in Raleigh, N.C. and the University of North Carolina in Chapel Hill, N.C. with a degree in Art Education. Before beginning her own agency in 1982, Martha taught art in Texas, Alabama, California, and Puerto Rico while her husband was in the Air Force. She and her husband have two grown daughters.

Typing by Jewell Robinson, Administrative Assistant with the North Carolina Global TransPark Education and Training Center, Kinston, N.C.

TarPar Ltd.

**1202 Harding Avenue
Kinston, NC 28501**

Other Titles Available

LISTEN by Fran Parker – A beautiful chapbook of art and prose that encourages the readers to take time to listen, enjoy life, and the total pleasures that each day offers. $8.00

PONDERINGS by Fran Parker – A heartwarming collections of prose and art that has been an overwhelming success. If you love the water, the sea and beautiful art...and have ever been in love...this is a must for your collection. $8.00

MUSHROOMS, TURNIP GREENS AND PICKLED EGGS by Fran Parker Don't be turned off by the title! This stand-by has been worth its weight in gold to many a new bride or the veteran cook. Three meals a day...365 days of the year...and recipes as needed, all planned for you along with many festive occasions. $6.00

WHAT IS IT AND WHAT DO I DO WITH IT? By Fran Parker and Beth Tartan. This is the perfect guide through housewares that helps every cook to learn what they are and how to use all the "gadgets" on the market, from the Aebeskiver Pan to a Zester, along with great recipes for each. $4.00

WHATS NEW IN WEDDING FOODS? By M. Sparks and Beth Tartan. If you have ever planned a wedding or have those thoughts running around in your mind, this book is a must! A complete guide to "doing" the wedding right and planned receptions to keep you on track. $4.00

Order from the above address. Enclose $1.45 per book for postage and .06% for N.C. tax. Satisfaction guaranteed. Gift wrapping and mailing to another address is $1.00 per book.

```
Any Organization that would like to
use any of the TARPAR LTD. books,
including JOY, for a fund raising
project should contact the above
address or call 252-523-5369.
```